THE BOY FRIEND

THE BOY FRIEND

A New Musical Comedy
of the 1920's

BOOK, LYRICS AND MUSIC BY

SANDY WILSON

PUBLISHED BY

CHAPPELL & CO., LTD.,

50 NEW BOND STREET, LONDON, W.1

TIME: 1926

ACT I

The Drawing Room of the Villa Caprice,
Madame Dubonnet's Finishing School, Near Nice.

Morning

———

INTERVAL

———

ACT II

The Plage

Afternoon

———

INTERVAL

———

ACT III

The Terrasse of the Café Pataplon

Night

"The Boy Friend" was originally presented at the Players' Theatre on 14th April, 1953. The first public presentation was at Wyndhams Theatre on 14th January, 1954, when the cast was as follows:

HORTENSE (*a French Maid*) .. .. VIOLETTA
MAISIE } *Pupils at* { .. .. DENISE HIRST
DULCIE } *Mme. Dubonnet's* { .. .. MARIA CHARLES
FAY } *Finishing School* { .. .. JOAN GADSDON
NANCY } .. .. JULIET HUNT
POLLY BROWNE .. .. ANNE ROGERS
MARCEL .. .. STEPHEN WARWICK
PIERRE .. .. JACK THOMSON
ALPHONSE .. .. GEOFFREY WEBB
MADAME DUBONNET .. .. .. JOAN STERNDALE BENNETT
BOBBY VAN HUSEN .. .. LARRY DREW
PERCIVAL BROWNE .. .. HUGH PADDICK
TONY .. .. ANTHONY HAYES
LORD BROCKHURST .. .. JOHN RUTLAND
LADY BROCKHURST .. .. BERYL COOKE
GENDARME .. .. HUGH FORBES
A WAITER .. .. ALAN DUDLEY
PÉPÉ } *Speciality* { .. ..STEPHEN WARWICK
LOLITA } *Dancers* { .. .. JOAN GADSDON
GUESTS .. .. STELLA CHAPMAN
ELEANOR McCREADY
ROBERT HARGREAVES

The part of Percival Browne was taken over in
May 1954 by Fred Stone

PRODUCED BY VIDA HOPE

Dances arranged by John Heawood

Scenery and costumes by Reginald Woolley

THE BOY FRIEND

MUSICAL CONTENTS

THE BOY FRIEND

SANDY WILSON

OVERTURE

N⁰ 1

Piano

44762

MADE IN ENGLAND

2

Valse con moto

Chappell

E Moderato *(rhythmically in 4)*

Chappell

4

Chappell

Act I

CHORUS OF GIRLS–(with Solo–Hortense)
"PERFECT YOUNG LADIES"

Nº 2

Note:– At curtain rise Piano (only) plays from 1st bar ad lib (under dialogue) till Cue

Cue: (GIRLS) "Of course not"

We're per-fect young la-dies Pre-par-ing to take ___ Our pla-ces a-mong the no-
per-fect young la-dies Who hope to at-tract ___ A hus-band whose cre-dit is

-blesse. ___ We're per-fect young la-dies Pre-par-ing to make ___
good. ___ (HORTENSE) You may be young la-dies But why don't you act ___

The most of the charms we pos-sess. ___ We're be-ing
The way that a young la-dy should? ___ I've of-ten

44762   Chappell

6

Dialogue
Chappell

No. 3   ENSEMBLE – (Polly, Dulcie, Fay, Maisie, Girls and Boys)

"THE BOY FRIEND"

Cue: (GIRLS) Oh, do tell us about him, Polly!

Moderato   A little faster

(POLLY) Well, there really isn't very much to tell. I expect you know how I feel as well as I do.

Polly

An-y girl who's reached the age Of sev-en-teen or there-a-bouts Has but one de-

POL

-sire in view. _____ She knows she has reached the stage Of

POL

need-ing one to care a-bout; No-thing else will real-ly do. _____

Chappell

8

Chappell

10 **D** 2nd CHORUS
Girls

We plead to have   We need to have   In fact our poor hearts bleed to have

That cer-tain thing called the Boy Friend.

We'd save for him   And slave for him   We'd ev-en mis-be-have for him

That cer-tain thing called the Boy Friend.

44762   Chappell

DANCE

mf a tempo

We're blue with-out   Can't do with out   Our dreams just won't come true with-out

That   cer - tain   thing   called   the   Boy   Friend.

(Dialogue)

№ 4   MADAME DUBONNET'S ENTRANCE

Cue: (MAISIE) "Cave, girls, here's Madame Dubonnet"

Moderato

(Madame D. sings melody, without words)

(Dialogue)

No. 5   DUET (Bobby and Maisie)

"WON'T YOU CHARLESTON?"

Cue: MAISIE. Really, I don't believe it.

 Chappell

C

A - round we will go, To - geth - er we'll show them How the ___
A - round we will go, To - geth - er we'll show them How the ___

Charles - ton is done. ___ We'll sur - prise ev - 'ry - one. ___
Charles - ton is done. ___ We'll sur - prise ev - 'ry - one. ___

___ Just think what Hea - ven ___ it's going to be
___ (BOTH) Just think what Hea - ven ___ it's going to be

If you will Charles - ton, ___ Charles - ton with me.
If you will Charles - ton, ___ Charles - ton with me.

 Chappell

Chappell

F

G

Meno mosso (*in 4*)

rall.

(Segue after applause)
Chappell

Nº 5a

REPRISE—(Bobby and Maisie)
"WON'T YOU CHARLESTON?"

Faster

Both

Won't you __ Charles-ton __ with me? _____ Won't you __

Charles-ton __ with me? _____ And while the band is play-ing that

Old vo - de - o - do. A - round we will go,

To-geth-er we'll show them How the__ Charles-ton__ is done.____

We'll sur - prise ev - 'ry - one._____ Just think what Hea - ven

it's going to be If you will Charles-ton, Charles-ton, Charles-ton,

If you will Charles-ton, Charles-ton__ with me!____

ff
(Drums ad lib.)

(Dialogue)
Chappell

№ 6   **DUET— (Madame Dubonnet and Percival)**

"FANCY FORGETTING"

Cue: Mme. DUBONNET "Let me see, how did it go?"

Chappell

Mme DUB: Fan - cy, just fan-cy you for - get - ting. _____

PER: Fan - cy, just fan-cy you for - get - ting. _____

Dialogue

№ 7

MELOS

POLLY'S LETTER

Cue: (POLLY) "Good-bye" (Girls exuent)

Moderato *(in 4)*

(Polly throws letter)

Tony enters - Dialogue

Chappell

Nº 8

DUET—(Tony and Polly)

* "I COULD BE HAPPY WITH YOU"

Cue: (TONY) "I think you're terribly" (POLLY) "Yes?"

Tony

I don't claim that I am psy-chic, But one look at you and I kick A-

(Orch. tacet Voice and Piano only)

TONY

-way ev-'ry scru-ple I learnt as a pu-pil In school, my dear.

Polly

I'm not one to make pre-dict-ions, But I've thrown off all re-strict-ions And

44762

Chappell

26

don't mind con-fess-ing I think it's a bless-ing That you are here.

Tony

Though I'm pre-pared to find I'm wrong, _____ I've got a fun-ny

rall.

A *(Not too fast)*

feel-ing we be-long To - geth - er. I could be hap-py with

you _____ If you could be hap-py with me. _____

Polly

_____ I'd be con-tent-ed to live an-y - where, _____

Chappell

28

44762   Chappell

Chappell

30

Chappell

FINALE- ACT I
REPRISE (Ensemble)
"THE BOY FRIEND"

Cue: (POLLY) "He's really arrived!"

Chappell

Chappell

End of Act I

№ 10

1st INTERMISSION

Chappell

Chappell

Act II

ENSEMBLE
"SUR LA PLAGE"

 Chappell

Dulcie

me? _____ But what - ev - er you do _____ When I'm

swim-ming with you, _____ Please re - mem - ber not to go too far. _____

Boys

_____ Though you may look cute _____ In your bath - ing suit, _____

We don't know who you are.

Chappell

Chappell

40

DANCE

Chappell

Chappell

DUET – (Tony and Polly)

"A ROOM IN BLOOMSBURY"

Cue: (TONY) "How ripping — So am I!"

Chappell

Polly

Tony

pa - lace is   So full of fal - la - cies.   That's   true.   I've

got a ve - ry diff - 'rent sort of scheme in mind,   It's just a

dream de - signed   For two.   Would you care to hear a -

Polly

- bout it, dear?   Would I care to? Can you   doubt it, dear?

Chappell

Chappell

D DANCE

p staccato

marc. la melodia

E

R.H.

staccato

f

Both

All we want is a   room in Blooms-bu - ry. _____

Segue at cue:-
Tony hand in pocket for key

Chappell

Chappell

Nº 13

SONG – (Hortense) with Ensemble
"IT'S NICER IN NICE"

Note:- *The orchestral parts are in* 2/4 *time*

Cue: (HORTENSE) "And I'm very proud of it, too."

Con vivo *(in 2)*

A

Hortense

I'm of - ten asked if I would like to tra - vel, And

HOR

vi - sit oth - er lands a - cross the sea, _____ But

44762

Chappell

Chappell

50

say it's love-ly when a Young la-dy's in Vi - en - na, But it's
peo-ple's one de - sire is To go to Bue - nos Air - es But it's

ni - cer, much ni - cer in Nice, In Am-ster-dam or
ni - cer, much ni - cer in Nice, The laws are ra-ther

Brus-sels The men have great big mus-cles, But they're ni - cer, much ni - cer in
vague in The town of Cop - en - hag - en But they're ni - cer, much ni - cer in

Nice. I've heard that the I - tal - ians Are ve - ry fond of
Nice. And some may like a flut - ter In Bom-bay or Cal -

Chappell

2nd time only

dal - liance, And they're al - so keen on it in Greece. But what -
- cut - ta, But they might have trou - ble with the p'lice. Oh, la, la! Oth - er

- ev - er they may say, This is where I want to stay, For it's so much
pla - ces may be fun, But when all is said and done It is so much

1 **Ensemble**

She says it's ni - cer, much ni - cer in Nice.

ni - cer in Nice.
ni - cer in

2

She says it's ni - cer, much ni - cer in Nice.

2 Some Nice.

poco accel.

52

Chappell

Chappell

54

some may like a flut-ter In Bom-bay or Cal-cut-ta, But they might have

some may like a flut-ter In Bom-bay or Cal-cut-ta, But they might have

trou-ble with the p'lice. Oth-er pla-ces may be fun, But when

trou-ble with the p'lice. Oth-er pla-ces may be fun, But when

Chappell

Dialogue

Chappell

56

N⁰ 14

SONG—(Madame Dubonnet and Percival)

"THE 'YOU-DON'T-WANT-TO-PLAY-WITH-ME' BLUES"

Cue: (PERCIVAL) "Yes, most definitely"

Blues tempo

44762

Chappell

B

Oh dear, I've got the you - don't-want - to - play-with-me blues.

Percival

Don't-want-to-

(a tempo)

It's clear I've got the you - don't-want-to-

-play-with-me blues.

-stay-with-me blues. I am so good

Don't-want-to - stay-with-me blues.

Mme DUB. At spreading mirth and joy. ___ But it's no good

Mme DUB. With such a sul-ky boy. ___ I try To play the game the oth - er

C

Mme DUB. fel-lows all choose _____ I sigh Be-cause you al-ways re-fuse.

Percival

The oth - er fel-lows all choose

Mme DUB. What is a girl to do

Chappell

Chappell

N 15

SONG—(Maisie and Boys)

"SAFETY IN NUMBERS"

Note:- The orchestral parts are in 2/4 *time*

Cue: (BOBBY) "Listen to me"

Chappell

64

C *2nd time-* **Boys**

MAI: safe - ty _____ in num - bers, _____ That's what I _____

MAI: _____ be - - lieve, _____ The girl who knows _____ A

MAI: lot of beaux _____ Is nev - er like - ly to grieve. _____

D

MAI: _____ The la - dy _____ who slum - bers _____ Is

p-f

44762

Chappell

Chappell

66

44762

Chappell

Dialogue

Chappell

№ 16

Cue: (POLLY) "What did I say?"

Andante moderato

Chappell

TON

one thing is clear as can be,_____ I know that I could be

Both

hap-py with you, My dar-ling, If you could be hap-py with.....

(Dialogue continues)

№ 16ª

Cue: (POLLY) "A thief! Oh, no,"

Andante moderato

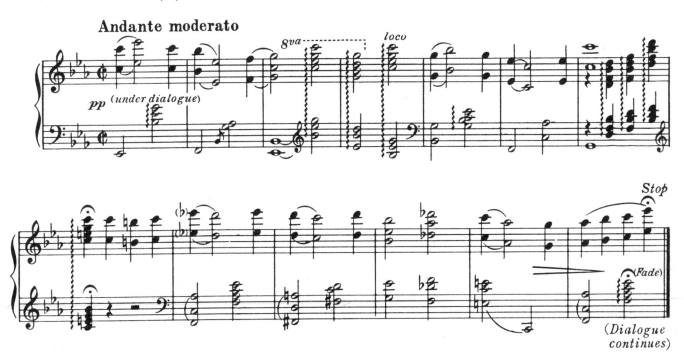

pp (under dialogue)

(Dialogue continues)

Chappell

Cue: (HORTENSE) "I think I can explain" ····

····"That men was Monsieur···   (POLLY) No! Hortense! You promised! (Mme. DUB) But what is it Polly?"

pp (under dialogue)

(POLLY) It's nothing, Madame, I'm just a little disappointed that's all. You see, I shan't be going to the Carnival Ball after all

rall.

Segue

Nº 16c

Polly

I could   be   hap - py   with   you,_____   If   you   could   be

mp (Piano only)   *8va*   *loco*

POL   hap - py   with   me._____   I'd   be   con - ten - ted   to

POL   live an - y - where_   What could I   care,—   As   long as   you were there?

(Orch. enters)

          Chappell

End of Act II
Chappell

№ 17

2ND INTERMISSION

In Bright 4

Chappell

C Fast *(in 2)*

(Orch. parts are in 2/4)

Segue

Chappell

OPENING ACT III

Stop at Cue:(PIERRE) "Regardez, regardez.... Mme. Dubonnet"

Chappell

№ 18ª

Cue: (LORD B.) "That's a familiar word"

Valse moderato

pp (under dialogue)

Fade at Cue: (Mme. DUBONNET) "Have some Champagne"

1 (Optional)

2

Chappell

Nº 18ᵇ

Cue: (PERCIVAL) "For that I shall always be grateful"

Valse moderato

Stop at Cue: (Mme. DUBONNET) "You said"

Chappell

Nº 18ᶜ

Cue: (PERCIVAL) "Yes! I'm beginning to remember"

Valse moderato

Nº 19

Cue: (BOYS) "How?"
(BOBBY) "We can ——

DUET — (Bobby and Maisie) with Chorus
"THE RIVIERA"

Chappell

Boys & Girls

And if you've had a tiff,— You'll soon for - get it, if— You

dance, you sim-ply got-ta dance._____

Here in the South of France They've got a new step._____

It's quite the cut - est dance In - vent - ed to step— So do step.

Chappell

B

ALL: Mul - ti - mill - ion - aires and their lit - tle pets do it.

ALL: Ev - en maid - en la - dies who wear lorg - nettes Have tak - en to it

ALL: Tell ev - 'ry-one to give out the news. This is the way to shake off the blues.

ALL: Ev - 'ry - bod - y's do-ing the Riv - i - er - a!

Chappell

Chappell

DANCE

E

(Segue after applause)

Chappell

REPRISE
"THE RIVIERA"

86

44762

Chappell

№ 20

TONY'S ENTRANCE

Cue: (HORTENSE) "Oh! Champagne!"

№ 20ª

TONY'S DANCE

Cue: (HORTENSE) "She may not come at all" (*Exit*)

Chappell

88

44762

Nº 21

DUET—(Lord Brockhurst and Dulcie)
"IT'S NEVER TOO LATE TO FALL IN LOVE"

Cue: (LORD BROCKHURST) "Yes, like me for instance"

44762

Chappell

Lord B. Al - though my hair is turn - ing grey. **Dulcie** Yes, it's ra - ther grey.

Lord B. I still be - lieve it when I say **Dulcie** Well, what *do* you say? **Lord B.** It's

Rhythmic *a tempo*
Lord B. nev - er too late to have a fling, For Au - tumn is just as

mf (Orchestra enters)

Lord B. nice as Spring, And it's nev - er too late to fall in

Chappell

 Chappell

they say I'm too old for you, Then I shall an-swer "Why, Sir, One

nev-er drinks the wine that's new; The old wine tastes much nic-er:" A

gent-le-man nev-er feels too weak To pat a pink arm or pinch a cheek, And it's

Sez who? Sez you?

nev-er too late to fall in love. Sez me Sez

DUL. Sez both of us to-geth-er. Con-

ord B. me, Sez both of us to-geth-er. It's nev-er too late to whis-per words

mf

DUL. -cern-ing the ways of bees and birds,

ord B. And it's nev-er too late to

DUL. Whack-a - do, Whack-a - do, Whack-a - do. It's

ord B. fall in love.

Chappell

Chappell

Segue after applause

Chappell

№ 21ᴬ

REPRISE
"IT'S NEVER TOO LATE TO FALL IN LOVE"

L'istesso tempo

Dulcie
It's nev-er too late to blow a kiss Es-

Lord B.
DUL. -pec-ial-ly at a time like this And it's nev-er too late to fall in

Dulcie
Vo-de-o, Vo-de-o, Vo-de-o.

Lord B.
love.
It's nev-er too late for

Chappell

fun and larks A jol-ly old flame has lots of sparks. And it's

nev-er too late to fall in love. The
Vo - de - o, Vo - de - o, Vo - de - o

mod - ern build - ings that you see Are of - ten most a - larm - ing
But

Chappell

98

Lord B. I am sure that you'll a-gree

Dulcie A ru-in—

Lord B. Can be charm-ing

Dulcie It's

DUL. nev-er too late to be a beau,

Lord B. Ex-pe-ri-ence counts a lot, you know

Both And it's

Both nev-er too late to fall in, nev-er too late to fall in,

Both nev-er too late to fall in love. _____

(Dialogue)

Chappell

No 22

CARNIVAL TANGO

Cue: (LADY BROCKHURST) "Revolting!"

Chappell

B a la Tango

C

gliss.

poco accel.

Drum roll

ff

sfz

(Dialogue)
Chappell

№ 23   **DUET—(Madame Dubonnet and Polly)**

"POOR LITTLE PIERRETTE"

Cue: (Mme. DUBONNET) "Yes, I think so"

Moderato

mf

poco rall.

Mme. Dubonnet

There is an old French leg-end That's set to an old French tune. It

mp colla voce
(Piano only)

tells how Pier-rot loved Pier-rette Un-der a sum-mer moon.

Ev-'ry night the lov-ers meet Just as the clock strikes nine.

R.H.

44762   Chappell

Then he gives her kis - ses sweet As vint - age wine.

But, a - las, one fate - ful night Pier - rette is for - sworn.

There she stands for - lorn Till the cold grey dawn.

A **With feeling** (*not too slow*)

Poor lit - tle Pier - rette, Where's your Pier - rot?

Chappell

Chappell

Chappell

Chappell

Dialogue
(almost Segue)

Chappell

Nº 24

PIERROT'S ENTRANCE

Cue: (Mme. DUBONNET)"Pierrot has not forgotten after all"

Dialogue

Chappell

№ 25   FINALE—ACT III (Ensemble)

Cue: (BOBBY) "Swell—now how about that Charleston?"

110

ENS Life with-out us is im-poss-i-ble And de-void- of all charms.

ENS No a-mount of i-dle gos-sip 'll Keep them out— of our arms

ENS We're blue— with-out, Can't do— with-out, Our dreams just won't come true— with-out

ENS That cer-tain thing called the Boy Friend.

rit.

Chappell

112

D

As long as you were there? Skies may not al-way be blue, _____ But

Broader

one thing is clear as can be, _____ I know that I could be hap-py with

rall. me. *Fine*

you, My darl-ing, If you could be hap-py with me, with me.

rall. *Fine*

44762

(*Segue after applause*)
Chappell

N° 25a

FINAL CURTAIN

Dal 𝄋 (page 111)
al Fine

N° 26

PLAY OUT

In Bright 4